THANK YOU

We want to thank all of the teachers, educators and children
who have inspired or maybe even created these ideas.

Thanks to the staff, parents and children of Peachtree Presbyterian Child Development Center,
Atlanta Georgia and Little Faces Learning Center, Atlanta, Georgia
for allowing us to play and photograph play in their programs.

Personal Thanks from Carole -
To Sweyden and my children, Arden, Christopher and Patrick
and my parents who didn't make me color in the lines.

Personal Thanks from Kathy -
Josh, thanks for having faith in me.
John Michael, you are the light of my world and I am thankful to be your mom.
Mom, Dad, Mandy, Brian & Doug, thanks for making life REAL!

Thank you God for our friendship and for the chance to make a difference.

Table of Contents

- idea #1 .... Corporate Elongated Strips of Paper
- idea #2 ...... Plungers Aren't Just For The Potty Anymore
- idea #3 .... The Jar
- idea #4 .... Shop 'Til You Drop
- idea #5 .... Clean Paint
- idea #6 .... Water Works
- idea #7 .... Tongue Painting
- idea #8 .... If The Shoe Fits
- idea #9 .... Squishy Squeezy
- idea #10 .... Ooey Gooey
- idea #11 .... Many Marbles Or Is It Mini Marbles?
- idea #12 .... Pull Out The Potting Soil
- idea #13 .... Bath Time
- idea #14 .... String Them Along
- idea #15 .... Wrap It Up
- idea #16 .... Cook Up Some Fun
- idea #17 .... See Spot Run
- idea #18 .... Take It Apart
- idea #19 .... Accordion
- idea #20 .... Stick With Color
- idea #21 .... Squirt It On
- idea #22 .... Fly Guts
- idea #23 .... Ice Sculpture
- idea #24 .... Ease That Easel On Outside
- idea #25 .... Planting Away The Day
- idea #26 .... The Key Idea
- idea #27 .... Put A Pencil To It
- idea #28 .... Tearing For Tantrums
- idea #29 .... HOT Plate
- idea #30 .... Shift The Sand Inside
- idea #31 .... Do Windows!
- idea #32 .... Stains To Shout About
- idea #33 .... Let's Go Swimming
- idea #34 .... Kitchen Gadgets
- idea #35 .... Popsicle Art
- idea #36 .... Construction Sites On The Move
- idea #37 .... Fly Paper
- idea #38 .... Hose 'Em Down
- idea #39 .... Dough Dough
- idea #40 .... Self-Portrait
- idea #41 .... Bubble Rap
- idea #42 .... Please Pass The Fish Sticks
- idea #43 .... Unload The Laundry
- idea #44 .... Smelly Smelly
- idea #45 .... Fort Building
- idea #46 .... Dress Me Up
- idea #47 .... Water Spectrums
- idea #48 .... Let's Go Camping
- idea #49 .... Paint The Town
- idea #50 .... Jump For Joy - It's Junk

Get Real
Get Messy

Ideas For Real Teachers

Carole H. Dibble ◆ **Kathy H. Lee**

Photography by Catherine Carr

Copyright © 1998, 1999 Early Childhood Resources Publishing, a division of Early Childhood Resources, LLC

All rights reserved. No part of this publication may be reproduced, stored in a retrieval system, or transmitted, in any form or by any means, electronic, mechanical, photocopying, microfilming, recording, or otherwise, without permission of the publisher.

Photographs by Catherine Carr
Cover Design by Anne Zafiroulis

Requests for permission to make copies of any part of the work should be mailed to Early Childhood Resources, 11770 Haynes Bridge Road, Suite 205-425, Alpharetta, Georgia 30004.

Address for orders:
Early Childhood Resources Publishing
11770 Haynes Bridge Road
Suite 205-425
Alpharetta, Georgia 30004
(770) 321-5494

ISBN 0-967087-0-6
Printed in the United States of America.

10   9   8   7   6   5   4   3   2   1

Table of Contents

idea #51	Stickers For Everyone
idea #52	Mystery Box
idea #53	It's A Wrap
idea #54	Bag It
idea #55	Don't Throw Those Markers Away
idea #56	Tell Me Your Story
idea #57	A Place For One
idea #58	Piece It Together
idea #59	Mississippi Mud
idea #60	Floaties
idea #61	Sticky Steppin'
idea #62	The Car Wash
idea #63	You Can Dance
idea #64	Coverings For Your Head
idea #65	Bring In The Bugs
idea #66	This Paint Smells
idea #67	It's Tool Time
idea #68	Brains?!?
idea #69	Paper Collage Minus The Paper
idea #70	Let the Sun Shine On Your Shoulders
idea #71	Cube Color
idea #72	Take Out The Crayons
idea #73	Reuse It
idea #74	What's In A Box
idea #75	The Taste Test
idea #76	Rain! Rain! Don't Go Away
idea #77	Memories...
idea #78	Rock n' Roll
idea #79	Making Tracks
idea #80	Bottles Of Stuff
idea #81	The Art That Keeps Going And Going
idea #82	The Ultimate Party Hat
idea #83	Splatter Paint
idea #84	Build Your Own House
idea #85	Box Blocks
idea #86	The Stocking Drop
idea #87	Without Form. But Not Without Purpose
idea #88	Magic Feathers
idea #89	Basic Bubbles Are A Blast
idea #90	Rover, Bring Me That Toy - I'm Painting
idea #91	Rainbow Flour
idea #92	Play In The Dirt Again... And Again...
idea #93	Prop It Up
idea #94	Oil And Water Don't Mix
idea #95	Dying Eggs In Septmber ???
idea #96	Glarch, Gak Or Whatever It Is Called
idea #97	Field Trips To You
idea #98	Tracks
idea #99	Textures To Touch
idea #100	Just Imagine...

FORWARD

This book is about helping teachers of young children provide experiences that are meaningful to children in the process of doing, rather than simply looking for an outcome or product. What a teacher believes about children is directly reflected in the activities they select for their classroom. If teachers believe children are incomplete, empty vessels waiting to be filled with knowledge, then success will be measured by the children's ability to repeat back what they are taught. We believe children come to this world as complete beings, ready and capable of constructing knowledge based on experience. This means children learn through daily experiences and processes.

We have written this book for the "real teacher", not afraid to let children explore and take charge of their own learning. Through process, teachers encourage children to think creatively, solve problems and discover the joy of learning.

Although we have laughed at ourselves and hope to make you laugh, we do take the work of working with children very seriously! We are passionate about our mission to improve the quality of care and experiences for young children. The objective of this book is to increase teacher awareness to the benefits of processes and inspire teachers to try new processes in their classrooms.

So — Let's Get Started!!!

Getting Started

- We wish we could say every idea in this book was our very own, created out of our very own heads, but it's not true.
- We wish we could say that we are truly famous and well respected scholars, but it's not true.
- We wish we could say that this book will solve every teacher problem, but it's not true.
- We can say we created a few of these ideas and have tried all of them, that's true.
- We can say we know some famous and well respected scholars and we hope they would approve of these ideas, that's true.
- We can say we tried to make this a fun and teacher-friendly book, that's true.
- We can say the process is more important than the product, **THAT'S TRUE!**

Personal Notes

idea #1

Corporate Elongated Strips Of Paper
(AKA - shredded paper from the office)

Get those parents to the shredder. Have them bring bags and bags of shredded paper from their offices. Set out lots (the more the better) of the shredded paper and let the children play in it, throw it, hide under it or anything else fun! After play, save a little for your next collage project.

Personal Notes

idea #2

Plungers Aren't Just For The Potty Anymore!!!

Plungers can be bought in many sizes. Let children paint by dipping new plungers into tempera and stamping the shapes on paper. The more choices of paint and the more choices of paper, the more individual the art will be. Plunge on!

> Being a kid teacher is dirty, messy, noisy, work.
>
> Carole Dibble

Personal Notes

idea #3

The Jar

Children tear small pieces (about 1" X 4") of the ever famous colored tissue paper. Dip the paper in glue and spread it across the outside of a jar. Layer the tissue paper on the jar, covering the entire jar for a beautiful creation. After the glue has dried you can help the children shellac their art to preserve its beauty. This is a really cool looking finish!

Personal Notes

idea #4

Shop 'Til You Drop

Ask parents to bring in shopping bags. The really cool paper kind with handles are fun! Place them in different interest areas and see how many uses the children think of for these bags. They will sort, store and carry all sorts of typical classroom things. They may even hide something in a bag.

Personal Notes

idea #5

Clean Paint

We know that teachers have been waiting for the perfect paint product that never stains, doesn't drip and entertains children for hours. We haven't invented this paint, but this is a pretty good idea. Let children mix up finger paint using liquid soap and powdered tempera. The soap makes clean up a breeze. This is the almost perfect finger paint!

Funny, but true story-

One morning Kathy walks by the toddler room and there stands Hays with just her diaper on painting herself red. Kathy said, "Hays, what are you doing?" Hays replied, "Painting myself red." Because Hays had touched it and experienced it, she understood the color red. I hope she was using clean paint. Dare to be bold!

Personal Notes

idea #6

Water Works

Water, Water, Water. Before your class heads outside, set out some buckets of water and some paintbrushes. Watch what happens when the children discover these goodies.

Wait until you see how many times we will mention water in this book?

Personal Notes

idea #7

Tongue Painting
(We didn't have to think of a clever title,
we already have your attention)

On a piece of paper, place 1 tablespoon gob of corn syrup. Add a drop or two of food coloring. Now using tongues, lick your way to a masterpiece worthy of any refrigerator!

You've got to be kidding!

Personal Notes

idea #8

If The Shoe Fits

Take dress-up to a whole new level by allowing children to try on each others shoes. Make sure you let them try your shoes on, too. Do the children think their shoes will fit like their friends? They will have fun comparing and contrasting their shoes to their friends' shoes.

Personal Notes

idea #9

Squishy Squeezy
(Can you say this ten times fast?)

Begin with a bag that really seals (we can't use the brand name or we might get in trouble, but it has the word zip in it). Now add shaving cream (we don't think shaving cream is a brand name). Now, squeeze it, squish it, change the color by adding tempera, and enjoy!

This is a low maintenance process, unless you forget to seal the bag!

> *Babies are such a nice way to start people.*
> — Don Herold

Personal Notes

idea #10

Ooey Gooey

Put several boxes of corn starch in your sensory table. Let the children play in the dry corn starch, experiencing the texture and consistency. Next, let the children add water to the corn starch. Encourage children to describe what happens. Talk about the change in the texture and consistency. Notice it feels firm to pick up and then seems to melt in your hands (unlike M & M's).

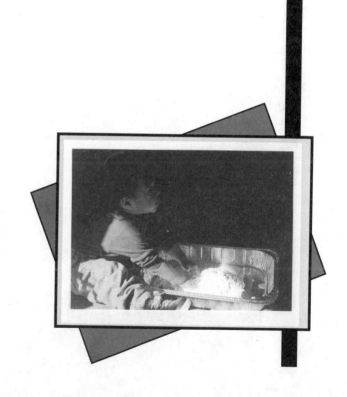

Personal Notes

idea #11

Many Marbles Or Is It Mini Marbles?

Put a piece of paper (any paper) in a box (any box). Next, add drops of paint (any paint, any color). Finally, add marbles (many marbles or mini marbles). The more marbles, the more fun! Roll 'em around and bounce 'em up and down! Now *this* is art!

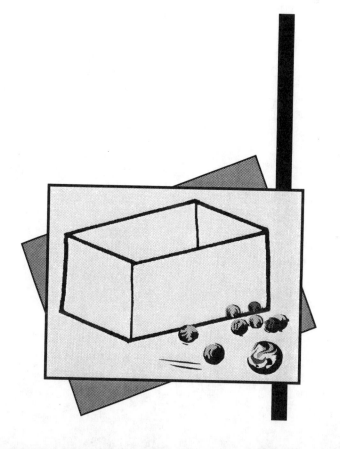

Personal Notes

idea #12

Pull Out The Potting Soil

Pour a bag of potting soil into your sand table or a large tub. Add cups, spoons, and shovels and you have a great digging area. You can even add pumpkin seeds or other kinds of seeds. Have the children bury the seeds in the soil. This is a super sensory activity. If you want to be really daring, add water!!!

> The purpose of play is to go out and be happy... to lay down cares and have fun for a while.
> — william Dorn

Personal Notes

idea #13

Bath Time

This isn't bath time for the children, although I bet some parents wish we would give them baths. Create soapy water in the sensory table and let the children bathe the baby dolls. This is a great way to get the dolls clean while the children have fun. Be sure to have plenty of towels on hand for the wet babies (we mean children and dolls)!

Personal Notes

idea #14

String Them Along

Give children string. Let them dip the string in globs of paint and swish them over the paper. Lots of colors will make lots of variety in the pictures. Different types of string will give different quality of lines. Once they have finished painting with the string, the strings can be pasted on a piece of paper for an entirely different look to string art.

> Children are the connoisseurs. What's precious to them has no price - only value.
>
> - Bel Kaufman

Personal Notes

idea #15

Wrap It Up

This idea is a super, appropriate, and practical gift for parents. Cut butcher paper or brown wrapping paper into various sizes. Have the children paint on the paper using hand prints or gadgets. Roll the paper up and tie a ribbon around it (after it has dried). Parents will enjoy wrapping presents as they show off their child's artwork with friends and family members.

Personal Notes

idea #16

Cook Up Some Fun

Children love to help out in the kitchen, but can we turn the cooking over to the children? Sure we can! Let each child use their own cutting board and a plastic knife to create a fruit salad extraordinaire. This means children do the cooking (not the teacher). Children can make their own soup, create their own pizzas, or shake up a milk shake. The whole idea is each child has created their own dish to enjoy!

Personal Notes

idea #17

See Spot Run

How many times has a child in your classroom blobbed on a gob of paint? The next time you find yourself in this predicament take advantage of the moment. Encourage the child to hold up the blobbed artwork and let the gobs run. You should, very quickly, put a piece of paper under the running paint to catch this new artwork in progress. This is two for one art!!

> *The possible's slow fuse is lit by imagination.*
> — Emily Dickinson

Personal Notes

idea #18

Take It Apart

What is it about children and their urge to "destroy" things? Why not help children curb this urge in an appropriate way? Ask parents to bring in broken household items, such as, phones, radios, bicycles, etc... Adding a repair shop to your "typical" learning areas can add real excitement and a new level of learning to your classroom.

Before long, parents might be bringing their cars in for tune-ups.

Personal Notes

idea #19

Accordion

(This idea came from Kathy Evins, a real teacher and this is her real idea!)

First, the children cut strips from a paper bag. Next they fold the strips accordion style. Now, they are ready to paint the strips with tempera. After the strips dry, they can glue them to paper or even use them with other collage materials to create their own multi-media creation.

This would be super to do when your class is reading Eric Carle books, he uses multi-media to create the art work.

Personal Notes

idea #20

Stick With Color

(This idea did not come from Kathy Evins, but she is still a real teacher!)

Tape comes in all colors. There is a whole palette of different tapes in different colors. And, oh, the uses! Children tape on the walls. Children tape on paper. Children tape on their clothes. Children tape on toys. Children tape on each other. Children tape on the floor. I think you get the point, they love to tape, and color only makes it cooler!

Personal Notes

idea #21

Squirt It On

Take several squirt bottles and mix water and tempera paint (liquid or powder). You should have several colors for the children to choose from. Place a large piece of paper on the easel and let the children squirt their way to beautiful art. For a different experience, hang a large sheet on the fence outside and let the children squirt away. This colorful sheet will make a cool back drop for your home living area.

> Never give up on a child.
> — *Patricia Willis*

Personal Notes

idea #22

Fly Guts

In a sensory table or a large tub, mix together shavings of ivory® soap, shredded toilet paper and water. Don't just use one bar of soap and a few sheets of tp, GO WILD!!! This is an activity where more is better.

Disclaimer: This activity is not for the weakened stomach

Personal Notes

idea #23

Ice Sculpture

Freeze water in old milk jugs with the tops cut off or in a bucket or pail. After the water freezes, dump the ice into a big wash tub. Children can create an ice sculpture using warm water in pitchers or pipettes. Melt your way to a new creation. Add food coloring or colored water to make it more interesting. We've been more successful at sculpting ice than sculpting our abs.

Imagination is the highest kite one can fly.

Lauren Bacall

Personal Notes

idea #24

Ease That Easel On Outside

This is another one of those ideas you wish you had written down. Drag that art easel outside. Provide plenty of paint, lots of paper and see what the children use as their paint brush. It may be a pine cone, a leaf or even their fingers. You might want to have paint brushes handy, just in case.

Personal Notes

idea #25

Planting Away The Day

Planting seeds is an excellent way to help children discover living things. This process can be as simple as planting a few seeds in a cup and watching them grow in your classroom window. For a process that is more involved, the children can grow an actual garden outside. Either way, the children will enjoy watching their gardens grow.

Personal Notes

idea #26

The Key Idea

Ask parents to empty their key rings and donate their keys. You know, all of those keys that they have no idea what they unlock. Put the keys on a ring and the children are ready to lock the door, drive to the store, open the gate or do any other number of things they have seen adults do with keys. Not only are keys for locking and unlocking, they are shiny and make a great jingle-jangle in pockets. This is the perfect object for fun!

Personal Notes

idea #27

Put A Pencil To It

Paper and pencils are not just for the Writing Center any more! Add a basket of paper, crayons and pencils to other interest areas and see how children decide to use it. They will think of many reasons to write throughout the day. Don't think toddlers are too young for this idea. They will "write" just like they see adults write. Just give them the opportunity and they will find a reason and a way to write.

Carole was observing in a classroom, using a clipboard and pen. Sarah approached and wanted to know what Carole was doing. Carole said, "I'm watching you play." Sarah said she wanted to watch too. She went to the writing center and got paper and pencil. The teacher noticed and got Sarah a clipboard too. Sarah sat just like Carole and "wrote" about kids playing. What a wonderful prewriting moment.

Personal Notes

idea #28

Tearing For Tantrums

We know that the little darlings in your class never throw a tantrum. But if a child should, this is a unique way for children to vent that anger. Provide the child a phone book (or piece of one) and let them tear away their frustrations by ripping the pages. Tearing paper is a pre-cutting skill and a terrific way to vent off a little steam.

(This could be a way for teachers to vent their frustrations, too.)

Personal Notes

idea #29

HOT Plate

Tomorrow, on your way to work, stop by your local home goods store and ask for lots of leftover tiles. Offer the tiles to the children as a canvas for their art process. The children can paint or print on the tile. Once the tile is dry, shellac the masterpiece and you have a super gift for mom and dad!

> If we allow children to show us what they can do rather than merely accepting what they normally do, I feel certain we would be in for some grand surprises.
> - *Mem Fox*

Personal Notes

idea #30

Shift The Sand Inside

Haul it in! Shovel it in! I know it sounds crazy, but it's fun! Bring in a pile of sand. Put it on a tarp or tile area. Add trucks, construction equipment and blocks. When children arrive in the morning, they will quickly say good-bye and come to join the construction crew working in the sand pile.

Personal Notes

idea #31

Do Windows!

We are not into child labor, but we are into child fun! Provide children with windows (any windows they can reach will do). Give them a pan of water, a sponge, and a squeegee. Put it all together and you have window washing at its finest, while having a blast! This is a super summer day experience.

Personal Notes

idea #32

Stains To Shout About

These stains are not on your clothes. These stains are made on paper using colored tissue scraps. Wet scraps of tissue paper. Then, drag, place or dump the wet tissue on a piece of paper. When you lift the soggy tissue, the colored stain is left behind. Children will shout with joy as they discover a whole new way to "paint" without paint!

Personal Notes

idea #33

Let's Go Swimming

It begins with a kiddie pool. It continues with *lots* of flavored gelatin, about 20 packs, made according to package directions. The flavor is not important, but the color is because it stains. We recommend lemon or another light color. Add the gelatin to the kiddie pool. Now, the slime begins. Be prepared with swimsuits, soap and a hose for kid clean up.

> This activity is special to Kathy because it brings back special memories of a special little boy named Michael Ghormley. Carole dreamed up this activity for summer camp. When we did it, we used orange jello. (Orange jello does stain). That night Michael spent the night with Kathy and wouldn't take a bath, he said he liked the color the jello made him. The next day he went to school all orange again.

Personal Notes

idea #34

Kitchen Gadgets

What can you do with all the stuff in your third from the left kitchen drawer? You know, the one with all the kitchen gadgets, just in case, like the sifter and the egg yolk separator. Add them to your art center and see the many uses the children discover for these gadgets. You'll wonder why you didn't think of it first!

Personal Notes

idea #35

Popsicle Art

Freeze tempera paint in ice cube trays. After 15 minutes, insert popsicle sticks. Continue to freeze until solid. Let children paint with these frozen treats. The more it melts, the more paint applied.

(These popsicles are for art processes only. They are not currently recognized by the USDA as a significant source of nutrition. They don't taste too good either.)

All art takes courage.
-Ann Tucker

Personal Notes

idea #36

Construction Sites On The Move

Bring those blocks outside for building with a whole new perspective. When children build with blocks inside, they are generally building on a flat, smooth surface. The ground outside gives your construction workers a whole new set of opportunities and challenges. Now, don't freak! The blocks will not get that dirty! Children can wash them in a tub of water as they come back into the classroom.

Personal Notes

idea #37

Fly Paper
(Not to be confused with Fly Guts, see **idea #22**)

Tack up a big sheet of butcher paper, spray on the 3M® Super 77 Adhesive spray and see what your children will "catch" on their sticky paper. They can add collage items, the ever famous tissue paper, family pictures, nature items, or anything else the kids can think of. They will be more creative than we could ever be.

Personal Notes

idea #38

Hose 'Em Down

This seems so simple, you are going to wish you had thought to write it down and become rich and famous like us. That's right, just pull that water hose out and have a good time. Spray 'em, squirt 'em and be sure to be prepared to get wet and have fun yourself!

Personal Notes

idea #39

Dough Dough

This is the dough recipe you always see in your resource books, but you can't ever find it when you need it. Combine 2 cups of flour, 1 cup of salt, 2 cups of water, 1 tablespoon of oil and 4 teaspoons of cream of tartar. Microwave on high, stirring after each minute until it is the correct consistency. In our humble opinion this is the best dough around!

Kathy wants to tell you to get parents to bring their old cookie cutters in to use with this dough.

Carole wants to tell you to get one inch thick dowels and have them cut about 6 inches long to use as rolling pins. (The kids can sand the ends in preparation for rolling).

Personal Notes

idea #40

Self-Portrait

Provide children with a full-length mirror so they can see themselves from head to toe. Supply paint and brushes and let children create their self-portrait directly on the mirror. They may want to paint their whole body or they may want to add features to their reflections. When they have finished painting, have a spray bottle ready for the little artists to clean the mirror for the next child.

Personal Notes

idea #41

Bubble Rap
Do The Bubble Wrap!

Resist the urge to pop the bubble,
if you pop then you're in trouble.
That bubble wrap has many uses,
we don't want to hear your excuses.

        Let the kids paint and print,
        this is more than just a hint.
        Bubble wrap is not lacking,
        it is more than just for packing.

Use the bubble wrap to make prints. Just paint on the bubble wrap and apply to paper for a print as original as this "Rap".

> Now that we know you better, we feel we can share with you. We sent this rap to a record company. I know you'll find this hard to believe (we did), but they turned us down. We will try to not let this effect our self esteem, but please... be kind.

Personal Notes

idea #42

Please Pass The Fish Sticks

Hands-on learning involves lunch and snack time, too. Food should be in containers that allow children to serve themselves in a relaxed family-style environment. Sure, they may get peas on the table, potatoes in their hair and spill their milk, but there is no reason to cry over spilled milk. Remember, it's the process not the product and patience is a virtue. You will be surprised how quickly they will catch on.

Personal Notes

idea #43

Unload The Laundry

You probably think laundry baskets are for carrying clothes. But no! They have so many more uses, according to some boys we know (John Michael Lee and Patrick Dibble). Laundry baskets make great animal cages, space ships, boats, and much more. Any size will do - tall, short, even the old broken ones work. Just bring on the baskets.

Personal Notes

idea #44

Smelly Smelly

What do you smell when you walk in your center? Does it make your nose turn up because it is clear that you do diapers? Does it smell of disinfectant and remind you of your pediatrician's office when you were a kid? Make the smells in your center pleasant for everyone by cooking up some cinnamon sticks in the kitchen, or using a bread machine to make bread in your classroom. This not only makes it smell good, but tastes great too.

> The succesful child is not the child that can memorize facts, but rather, the child that can ask the winnowing question.
> - *Jane Healy*

Personal Notes

idea #45

Fort Building

You don't have to be a master builder to have fun creating a fort. It only takes wood, nails, saws, hammers and safety gear. Many home goods stores that cut wood for customers, have scraps they will donate. You provide the rest. Let the kids plan and create their own forts. The children will have fun putting the wood together and building it themselves.

Personal Notes

idea #46

Dress Me Up

Pack the clothes away for the day and break out your leftover fabric, sheets, table cloths or sashes. The children will tailor clothes to their own taste as they drape, wrap, and tie themselves. These designers will be ready to show their wares at your next classroom fashion show.

Who knows, you may want them to design your next party attire.

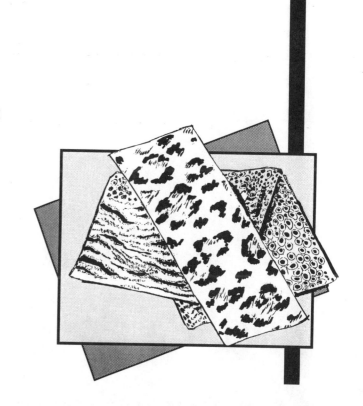

Personal Notes

idea #47

Water Spectrums

Have parents complained about the stains from food coloring that sometimes linger after an art process? Here's a simple solution that costs only pennies to make! Add a couple of teaspoons of liquid tempera to a bottle. Next, add water. Continue to add paint until you have the color you want. It's safe! It's washable! It's affordable! Another parent crisis solved!

> Educating the child begins with educating the parent.
>
> — Kathy H. Lee

Personal Notes

idea #48

Let's Go Camping

Bring the tent out of the wilderness and into the classroom. The ideas are endless. It makes a great "place for one" or a fun place to have lunch. A child might climb in with a book or maybe a bunch.

WATCH OUT - If your co-workers are missing, they might be napping in the tent!

Personal Notes

idea #49

Paint The Town

How cool do kids think the house painter is? After all, they do get to use all of that cool painting equipment. You can be a hero in your class by letting everyone use that cool painting equipment. Just bring in some paint rollers and buckets and your ready to paint the town. (No paint necessary.)

Personal Notes

idea #50

Jump For Joy - It's Junk

Oh, the treasures to be found at the junkyard! How about an old tub as a place for one or a unique sensory area? What could the children do with a few spare car parts like hubcaps or a steering wheel. The junkyard is a field of dreams (and good stuff) for the resourceful teacher.

Personal Notes

idea #51

Stickers for Everyone

Kids love stickers! Have them available all over the room. Have them in the art area, in home living, in the science area, in the math area (great for patterns), and definitely near the mirror to be applied directly to children. Yes - they will decorate the mirror and the classroom with these stickers. How great is that?!?

> *Promising goodies to children for good behavior can never produce anything more than temporary obedience.*
>
> *- Alfie Kohn*

Personal Notes

idea #52

Mystery Box

Kids go crazy when you bring out something new for the room. With a mystery box, it is easy to capture children's interest. Use a decorative box and fill it with different items each week. Some suggestions for your box include: pine cones of all shapes and sizes, an assortment of buttons, or zippers, or things that are red.

Personal Notes

idea #53

It's A Wrap

Calling all parents! After those big gift-giving events, the children can use those leftover rolls of wrapping paper. Children always want to help wrap presents. Create a gift wrapping center complete with old rolls of wrapping paper, boxes, bows and don't forget the tape. The great news is... no one has to wait for the special event to open their present.

Personal Notes

idea #54

Bag It

This is another activity using those bags that seal really well, but we don't want to mention them by name (if you don't know what we mean, see **idea #9**). In one of "these" bags, place a big blob of finger paint. Now seal the bag!!!! Children can draw in the paint, using their fingers or other rounded, dull objects. It's fun to refrigerate before painting to add a whole new dimension to this process.

This picture has nothing to do with this activity. We just liked the picture.

Personal Notes

idea #55

Don't Throw Those Markers Away

I know you think those dried out markers are ready to trash, but don't be too hasty. Provide children with paper, cups of water and dried out washable or watercolor markers. Now they are ready to draw. Just dip the tip of the marker in the water and you're ready to do a lovely water color drawing.

Shhh- Don't share this idea too quickly. Just offer to take those old markers off of your fellow teachers hands!

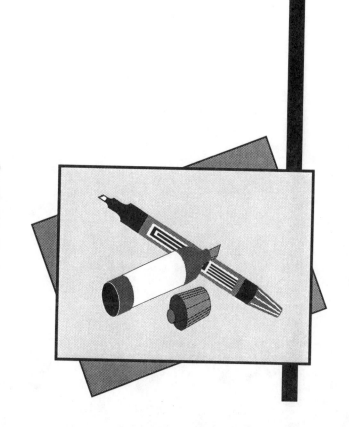

Personal Notes

idea #56

Tell Me Your Story

Kids love to talk. You can record a child's conversations on paper or you can set up a tape recorder, complete with microphone. Allow children to make their own tape of their voices. They can tell a story, sing a song or just talk, talk, talk. A copy of this tape would make a great present for parents. These tapes are great for the listening center, too.

Personal Notes

idea #57

A Place For One

Bring in that big appliance box, bring out the tempera, provide some paint rollers and make that box a home. Add pillows and a soft blankie and this is a great place to relax and get away from it all. But don't limit yourselves, tomorrow this home may be flying to Mars. Imagination is an amazing thing.

> Above all let children know you love them, no matter what.
> - Angela Stewart

Personal Notes

idea #58

Piece It Together

Give children a piece of cardboard cut to make a picture frame. Provide children with jigsaw puzzle pieces (the 445 pieces you can find of the 500 piece puzzle) and glue. Let children paste the puzzle pieces on to the card board. They can glue on as many pieces as they want. After the glue dries, children can paint the frame and you're ready for the perfect picture!

Personal Notes

idea #59

Mississippi Mud

(We both grew up in Mississippi so we named this activity in honor of the home state)

If you have been digging in the dirt lately, you may have noticed not all dirt is created equal. It comes in all sorts of shades and colors. Let children mix water with different shades of dirt to create different shades of paint. Then, create a really earthy picture full of dirt.

(Katherine Carr, the photographer for this book, is also from Mississippi.)

Facts About Mississippi

* Capital City: Jackson
* State Flower: The Magnolia
* State Bird: Mockingbird
* Elvis Presley was born in Tupelo and so was Carole.
*Kathy thinks Mississippi State is the greatest school!

Personal Notes

idea #60

Floaties

It is time to pull out those bags again that we don't want to mention by brand name, but we think you know what we mean (see **ideas #54 & #9**). Add water, sequins, confetti, and other floatable fun stuff. Seal carefully! This is a no mess activity, unless the bag comes unsealed and then you can call this a water activity!

> Those who know how to play can easily leap over the adversities of life.
>
> *- Iglulik Proverb*

Personal Notes

idea #61

Sticky Steppin'

Pull out that contact paper, but not for laminating. It is time to get steppin' on that sticky stuff. Tape the contact paper on the floor, sticky side up. Let the children walk across the contact paper (with shoes on or off). The children get such a kick out of sticking to the paper. It is also fun to watch the children discover that the paper is not sticky forever.

Every day's a kick!
- Oprah Winfrey

(A fellow Mississippian)

Personal Notes

idea #62

The Car Wash
(School Van or Bus)

When you were a kid, did you think it was the greatest to help wash the car? What a way to complete a field trip! Let the children wash the van. Provide those buckets, a little soap, a hose or buckets of water, a sponge and some rags for drying. You better watch out, the kids will want to start their own business.

Personal Notes

idea #63

You Can Dance

That's right! Put on the music and dance. It's great for the body and the soul. Party stores have great dance tunes or pull out your favorites from high school. Whatever the beat, the kids will join in.

> The children dance and the grown people get dizzy.
>
> *-anonymous*

Personal Notes

idea #64

Coverings For Your Head

Kids love to put things on their heads! Provide lots of different hats or even a bucket or two and watch children transform into a cowboy, a construction worker, a bride or maybe an ailien. You might have a special hat day where children wear in their favorite hat from home. Don't limit yourself to the traditional classroom hats, any funny hat will do.

Personal Notes

idea #65

Bring In The Bugs

That's right! Send the children out with small plastic bottles or ziploc® bags, maybe even a butterfly net. They will come back with living and dead treasures of bugs. Have plenty of magnifying glasses on hand for the children to check out their "finds" up close.

(Yes, we finally gave in and said the word. Ziploc® is a registered trademark of the Dow Chemical Co.)

Although some children would think this is a great activity, other children are not fond of bugs. Honor children's feelings when planning. John Michael, Kathy's son, does NOT like bugs. On the other hand, Christopher, one of Carole's sons, thinks bugs are great and is the first to spot a bug and get down to check it out more closely.

Personal Notes

idea #66

This Paint Smells!!!

We're not talking about the time you left the paint in the pot too long. Gross! Next time you put fresh paint in those pots, add a little baby powder for a new, and improved scent. But don't stop there. Try other good smells like vanilla or lemon extract. You might even explore with spices. Painting is now more than just for the eyes.

> Being a kid is dirty, messy, noisy work!
> - Carole Dibble

Personal Notes

idea #67

It's Tool Time

Kids love to put on a tool belt. I don't know why, I just know it's true. Some large home improvement stores sell kid size tool belts, but you could make your own with a strip of fabric for the belt and something to create loops for hanging tools. Your handy helpers help to keep the classroom looking new.

Personal Notes

idea #68

Brains?!?

Dissolve 16 packets (4 boxes) of knox® gelatin into 11 cups of water. Heat on stove while stirring constantly (not necessary to heat to boiling, a couple of minutes will do). Pour into two tubs (like cool whip® tubs). Chill until firm (the freezer works if you're in a hurry). Dump onto a washable surface and provide children with colored water and pipettes. Soon, you'll see why it is called brains.

> You never can tell when you do an act, what the result will be.
> - Ella Wheeler

Personal Notes

idea #69

Paper Collage Minus The Paper

Go ahead, put out the collage materials, but put the paper on the shelf. These collages are paper free and 3-D. It takes collaging to a new dimension - Children create sculptures, not just pictures.

> We must do the things we think we cannot do.
> *- Eleanor Roosevelt*

Personal Notes

idea #70

Let The Sun Shine On Your Shoulders

Head 'em up and move 'em outs. Take those sketch pads or paper out with colored pencils. The children will surely be inspired by the colors, smells, and sounds of the big outdoors as they draw and write on their pads. The colors of the different seasons provide a variety of different inspirations for the budding artists.

Personal Notes

idea #71

Cube Color

Start out with sugar cubes. Provide children with colored water made from food coloring and droppers or pipettes. Children will do the rest. They may stack and color. They may just color. No matter how children do it, discoveries are on the horizon.

> There is nothing like a group of four year olds to bring one down to normal size.
> -Docia Zavitikovsky

Personal Notes

idea #72

Take Out The Crayons

Next time you head outside for a walk, bring along the crayons and paper. Take a break in a shady spot and allow children to make crayon rubbings of objects in the great outdoors. Be sure and bring plenty of paper and different color crayons because the children will not want to stop with just one creation.

A curriculm geared to the needs of learners requires of the teacher an enormous amount of flexibility, a tolerance for unpredictably and a willingness to give up absolute conrol.
— Anonymous

Personal Notes

idea #73

Reuse It
(Not to be confused with Renuzit®)

We aren't talking your basic recycling here! We don't mean just toilet paper rolls. We are talking serious reusing and recycling. Contact large industries in your area and ask for their leftovers and discards. You'll be amazed at the findings, like plexiglass, labels, and newsprint rolls from the local newspaper. We even got a trap door from a bus, once!

> There is a use for almost anything.
> - George Washington Carver

Personal Notes

idea #74

What's In A Box???

Provide children with a box (a big box, a little box, a rectangle box, a square box). The children can begin personalizing their box with paint. After the paint dries, the process continues... gluing, stamping, taping, cutting, pasting, drawing, and whatever else the children desire.

BEWARE: This box may come to life!

Personal Notes

idea #75

The Taste Test

How many of you eat persimmons? Or when was the last time you had a pommegranite? It has probably been awhile. There are many different foods that are accessible for tasting. You may even find your grocer is willing to give you fruit at a discount if it been on the shelf for a day or two. Join in on the tasting. You might discover something delicious.

> **We may misunderstand, but we do not misexperience.**
>
> -Vine Deloria

Personal Notes

idea #76

Rain! Rain! Don't Go Away!

This is the perfect rainy day activity. Is there a rule written down anywhere that says children may NOT go outside in the rain? We say throw convention aside and head for the outdoors, even in the rain (but not the thunder and lightning). Let children sprinkle powdered tempera paint on plain paper. Then put on those raincoats and goulashes and head outside for the perfect water to complete the picture. Let the raindrops do all the work.

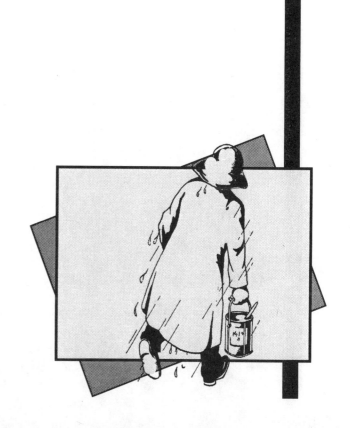

Personal Notes

idea #77

Memories...
(light the corner of your room)

So what do you do with all those pictures you make during the year? What about the menu from the class field trip or the tickets from the puppet show? What *is* a teacher to do with all this stuff? Make a memory wall. Take an area of your room and devote it to memories. Display pictures and keepsakes from field trips, parties and everyday events.

> *Traditions are the coat racks on which you hang your memories.*
> — Carolyn James

Personal Notes

idea #78

Rock n' Roll

Put on your walking shoes and head outside to fill those pockets with rocks. Have each child empty their pockets into their own shoe box. Add a little bit of paint and slice of paper. Place the lid on the shoe box, turn on Chuck Berry and *rock n' roll*. The children will enjoy shaking their box to the rhythm of the music. Take the lid off and discover what a little *rock n' roll* can do for your classroom.

Personal Notes

idea #79

Making Tracks

Start with a play car, dip the wheels in paint and *Make Tracks* on paper. Children can use different cars and colors, comparing the tracks or have tracks running in many directions. They can match the color of the car to the paint for a matching experience. This is a great activity for teachers to help young children build vocabulary as the children describe the cars and the tracks.

Personal Notes

idea #80

Bottles Of Stuff

Save your diet coke®, gatorade® and water bottles (any plastic bottle will do). Fill the bottles with a variety of materials (corn syrup, sequins, bells, confetti, little cars, oil, water, colored water, beads, etc.) Super glue the lid on the bottle and you have a variety of new toys for your classroom.

When Kathy adopted her son, John Michael, one of the teachers in the school gathered confetti from the shower and ribbons from the gifts and made a special bottle for John Michael. This was one of his favorite things to play with as a baby and now he loves to hear the story of his bottle.

Personal Notes

idea #81

The Art That Keeps Going And Going

Just when you think nothing can last a whole day, give this one a try. Tape a large piece of butcher paper on the wall or the floor. Put a bucket of crayons beside the paper and let children draw and color whenever they want throughout the day. As parents pick up, point out today's art work. No special display or assembly required.

Personal Notes

idea #82

The Ultimate Party Hat

Start with plain, colored party hats (the cheap, non-licensed, non-character ones). Provide children with typical collage materials, such as, buttons, fabric strips, the ever famous colored tissue paper, feathers, and anything else you have hanging around that you just won't throw away. Let the children decorate the hats as they please. Every child has their very own, unique, one-of-a-kind party hat!

Personal Notes

idea #83

Splatter Paint

(This was one of Carole's favorite things to do when she was four years old)

To make a splatter screen, attach screening material to a frame. Collect objects from nature and place them under the screen and on top of a piece of paper. Use a stiff-bristled brush (like a toothbrush) to rub paint over the screen. A really cool recessed design will appear on your paper.

> FIND SOMETHING YOU ARE PASSIONATE ABOUT AND KEEP TREMENDOUSLY INTERESTED IN IT.
> -Julia Child

Personal Notes

idea #84

Build Your Own House

Collect all of those empty cartons and boxes from your favorite foods and household items. Use a hot glue gun to put them together to make a room or maybe an entire house. When you move this building into the classroom, children will quickly make this house a home.

(This house makes a great space for one)

> It is crucial to always respect the homelife and daily experiences of those around us. Any time we deliver statements of judgement, others around us may incidentally hear our judgement and feel judged. It is important to be sensitive to and respectful of everyone's home and family lifestyle. Acceptance breeds self-esteem in children.
>
> - Carole Dibble

Personal Notes

idea #85

Box Blocks

Do you need new blocks in your room? Reuse your Capri Sun® boxes (or other small, sturdy boxes), add a little contact paper or paint and build your way to a new tall tower.

(Your director will love you for all the money you are saving on supplies because you are using recyclables!)

Knox Blocks

Here is a neat treat to have while playing with *box blocks.*

Dissolve four packages of flavored gelatin and one package of Knox® gelatin in four cups of boiling water while stirring. Chill until firm and cut into shapes.

Personal Notes

idea #86

The Stocking Drop

Using old stockings, fill the toes with sand or other objects. Small balls or marbles work great. Knot the open end. Dip the filled stockings in tempera. Now, drop the stockings on large butcher paper. A variety of colors may be used for a livelier look. Older children may want to see how changing the height from which the stocking is dropped changes the size of the image created on the paper.

Personal Notes

idea #87

Without Form, But Not Without Purpose

Give children sponges to paint with that have no special shape. Allow them to dip the sponges in globs of tempera paint and sponge the paint onto paper. The purpose of the activity is NOT to learn shapes, colors or print the shape of the theme of the week. The purpose is for children to experiment with color and texture and to create a truly original work of art.

> Like snowflakes, no two children are alike.
> - Theresa Walker

Personal Notes

idea #88

Magic Feathers

Bring on a tub of feathers. Have a large turkey baster with them. Children squeeze the turkey baster and release. Magically, feathers disappear. Children love to make things "disappear". As they squeeze in the feathers, they can count or wonder at how this magic works. Wow!

(Be on the look out! We hear this is how several professional magicians got their start.)

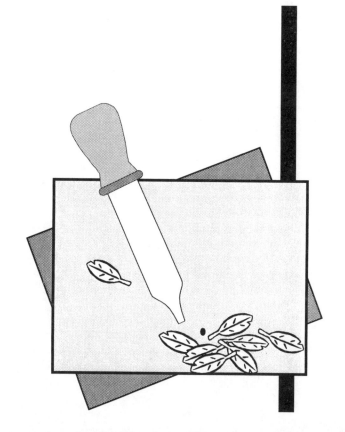

Personal Notes

idea #89

Basic Bubbles Are A Blast

Mix water and Dawn® dishwashing detergent to create your own bubbles. Try placing your bubbles in a small swimming pool and use hula hoops as bubble wands (very cool!). If you find yourself without bubble wands, don't fret... make a circle by placing your two hands together, thumb to thumb and pointer to pointer. Presto! It's a human wand.

Personal Notes

idea #90

Rover, Bring Me That Toy - I'm Painting

What a way to add variety in your art area. Pet toys offer many different shapes, sizes, and textures for children to experience. Dog bones are also fun for children to paint with. Your local dollar store should help you stock up on pet supplies for just a few bucks.

> Neither of us have a pet named Rover. Kathy has a dog named Kirby and Carole has a cat named Sassy.
>
> Update since the first edition - Now, Carole has the dog named Kirby and the cat named Sassy and Kathy has a cat named Fred that insists on living with her.

Personal Notes

idea #91

Rainbow Flour

Start with those handy dandy spray bottles and a tray of flour (cake flour or self-rising will do). Fill the spray bottles with various shades of colored water (**idea #47**). Encourage children to squirt the colored water on the tray of flour (verses the teacher) to experience the change that takes place when water and flour collide.

> Do you remember the first time you spotted a rainbow? What memories does this bring back for you? Take the time to share these memories with the children and help them create their own rainbow memories. You may find your classroom has its own rainbows when the light reflects into your classroom window in just the right way.

Personal Notes

idea #92

Play In The Dirt, Again ... And Again ... And Again!

When was the last time you baked up a delicious mud pie? Why not pull out those pie pans, pull up your favorite dirt pile and bake up super fun. Add a little water, lots of time to play, a warm day and imagination. You're sure to make culinary history!

Personal Notes

idea #93

Prop It Up

It starts with long tubes. Where do you get those? See **idea #73**. Now give them to the children and just let their imaginations soar. Challenge the children to use the tubes and props and think of all of the things the tubes can be (yes, they may be swords). Props are a great way to get imaginations in high gear and can prompt some interesting stories.

> *The social life of a child starts when she is born.*
> -Susanna Millar

Personal Notes

idea #94

Oil And Water Don't Mix

This one is such an old idea, it was around even before you were born. The truth is times have changed but this fact remains the same. Put out a pan with water. Have the oil ready to add. Kids are always amazed that it just won't mix. Let them add a little food coloring to really shake things up.

> Take time to laugh - it is the music of the soul.
>
> - *anonymous*

Personal Notes

idea #95

Dying Eggs in September???

Children LOVE dying eggs. It doesn't seem fair that children only get to dye eggs in the spring time. Dare to be different, let the children dye eggs throughout the year. Have an egg hunt. Read the story of humpty dumpty and let the children make their own humpty dumpty out of *boiled* eggs.

You can use a raw egg when telling the story of humpty dumpty, but remember that raw eggs contain salmonella, so wash your hands thoroughly with anti-bacterial soap.

Personal Notes

idea #96

Glarch, Gak Or Whatever It Is Called

In a container, pour in glue and liquid starch. Stir, add some more starch or glue, stir some more. Continue this process until you have a putty like consistency. You can refrigerate it, add color to it, or just play with it the way it is. Oh yeah, don't forget to name it.

(Kathy says, if it's stringy, you need more glue and if it's sticky, you need more starch. By the way, she calls it glarch.)

Personal Notes

idea #97

Field Trips To You

There are so many obstacles to field trips - the bus breaks down, not enough parent volunteers, we have to load all of those car seats into the van. Here's an alternative that eleminates so many of these headaches. Bring the field trip to your class. Some of our favorite field trips to bring into the classroom are the plumber, the landscape folks with their blowers, and the dog groomer. There are definitely others that have professions enormously interesting to preschoolers.

> Beauty in its truest form, is seeing the world through my child's eyes: seeing the excitement, the wonder, and the innocence. When I allow myself to do that, I am my happiest.
> - Laurie Numedahl-Meuwissen

Personal Notes

idea #98

Tracks

Little feet are s-o-o-o cute. Let those little feet create while they feel the squish-squash of paint between their toes. After they remove their shoes, let children step in the tempera paint and then walk across the butcher paper creating sweet foot prints. This is a mural parents are sure to appreciate.

Personal Notes

idea #99

Textures To Touch

Give children a piece of clear contact paper. Peel the backing, leaving the sticky side up. Provide a variety of collage items (buttons, feathers, confetti, sequins, colored tissue paper, etc.) and children will place them on the sticky surface. Fold over to seal this beautiful collection of treasures. This is fun to look at and to touch!

> I touch the future. I teach! (I mold and create too.)
>
> *Avisia Whiteman*

Personal Notes

idea #100

Just Imagine...

This is the best idea in the book. Don't limit yourself to these ideas. Go back to your childhood. What did you enjoy? What was your favorite thing to play? With a little imagination, you can bring these experiences to your classroom for your children.

Imagination is only intelligence having fun.

-George Sciabble

Personal Notes